... trip in to more
natural realities!

M........ 2022

Philly PA

TRAVEL BY HAIKU: VOLUMES 1 - 5

STILL TRIPPIN' ACROSS THE STATES

MARSHALL DEERFIELD

spread it

A FREEDOM BOOK

Published by A FREEDOM BOOKS

LIBRARY OF CONGRESS CATALOGUING IN PUBLICATION DATA
Kavanaugh, Marshall James, 1987-
Travel By Haiku: Volumes 1-5, Still Trippin' Across The States
/ Marshall James Kavanaugh
p. cm.
ISBN 978-0-6926-4879-7
1. Kavanaugh, Marshall James, 1987- -Biography.
2. Authors, American—21st century—biography

Printed in the United States of America

contact@marshalljameskavanaugh.com
www.marshalljameskavanaugh.com

Contents

Author's Note

Writing haikus began as a meditation on grounding myself in my surroundings as I traveled across the country. With each new town, campsite, or road stop, my mind faced the difficult prospect of trying to keep up. Here were new communities each with their own individual self-expressions, new landscapes as far as the eye could see, and countless incredible sunsets so unique in their vibrant colors. Even with this beauty right in front of me it was a battle just to keep my mind present and not hundreds of miles behind.

I wanted to be here now for all of it and not miss a single beat, distracted by my phone or following some tangential thought to carry me some other which way. By simplifying my own observations into the traditional haiku 5-7-5 algorithm, I found that quiet of mind that I so desired.

Suddenly time began to expand into much tinier even-more focused fragments. Rather than just seeing the warm day in front of me, I started to notice the way the sunlight caught the leaves of a nearby tree waving in the wind. My ability to sit with a waterfall and hear its voice/s became so overwhelming I almost began to understand what it all said. Bird songs became a language of where I was and what type of new magic awaited me and the more I listened, the more they glided into my vision.

Just like that I was addicted, the haikus quickly becoming a test or a game of my experience. Ask anyone who has traveled with me and they'll share with you several haikus we wrote together, scribbled in their own notebooks or stored away in their smart phones. The communal form probably stems from a haiku's simplicity. Something most of us are taught by some eccentric fifth grade teacher, unfortunately at an early age it's taught without the patience for the accompanying Zen mysticism. It also says something to this that the haiku's initial invention came out of a drinking game at the local dharma-bum cafés in 17th century Japan. Whatever it was, my practice continued to expand outwards and more and more people knew me for my haikus more than any of my other forms of writing.

Eventually, I began to share these short

meditations as little boosts over social media for friends back home. Little boosts meaning, ways of transporting my friends' collective consciousness out of the office spaces, out of the bedrooms, out of the subway stations, and into these surreal dreamscapes I was finding myself in. Little boosts to brighten their days. Little boosts to make the gray go away. Little boosts to make them think more about their planet. Little boosts to encourage them to let go and depart on similar wanderings.

The following book is a collection of those travels.

It is written in the spirit of a traveling Zen bard's name that I found on a road sign in the setting sun of Wisconsin on the way to Minneapolis, where two towns *Marshall* and *Deerfield* collide.

It is the whittled down form of hundreds and maybe thousands of haikus I wrote while I wandered.

It is a collected boost to be shared and devoured.

The book was cut up, re-bound, rearranged, tossed and turned, and finally arrived at five sections based on the location and general vibration of the pomes that migrated onto the page. Some haikus will read more like blips on a map that provide a summary description of my surroundings. Others will hopefully work to capture the essence of a moment as seasons change between spring and summer. Finally, there are a handful of haikus within these volumes that I hope caught some divine truth only visible when the mind stills, the stars come out bright, and one is completely alone with themselves and their universe.

Please read this book and feel its urgent call. There is much magic that awaits us when we go out into the world and pay attention. With more and more wilderness disappearing every year as humans keep expanding their civilizations, this magic disappears too. We must become connected again with our planet. We must become connected again to our inner spirits. Without this experience, we risk losing it all.

I hope you enjoy reading this book and the words become a part of your own meditation, serving to inspire, transporting us into higher realms, and leading the charge to fight for our mother Earth into the future. She needs us now more than ever.

Marshall James Kavanaugh
Philadelphia, PA
March 2016

Introduction

$$V(x,t) = A\sin(kx - \omega t + \theta)$$

"Two waves with the same frequency, wavelength, and amplitude traveling in opposite directions will super pose one another and produce a standing wave"

While reading *Travel By Haiku: Volumes 1-5* by Marshall Deerfield, I had some insight into the standing wave that Deerfield created while traveling, as if as a sound wave emitting from a guitar string set between the East and West coast, between the high and low octaves on the fret board of this landscape. Yet, it didn't stop there. These haikus reverberate so many standing waves:

- The wave like ridges of the mountains etching their sturdy spines into the sky.
- The waves of invisible air that trace their way in the sands of the deserts of the Southwest.
- The waves that ripple and lap the shorelines of the Pacific coast.

- The waves of fraternal sibling-hood within humanity cloistered and scattered across the country like grains of sand in wind.
- The waves of sunrises and sunsets that kiss and fall and rise with each day.
- The waves of breaths that we take that are given to us by the likewise breaths of the mighty trees and plants.
- The waves of a television that may speak of a vibe elsewhere and otherwise.

Tune in to these haikus and stories that paint an experience of reality that is vibing real hard, and everywhere.

Marshall Deerfield oscillates between the geologic scale of beauty and the breath of life that we take each moment, and may be too ensconced in the particular waves of our own storylines, shorelines, and horizons to take a moment, or twenty, to step back and behold!

As a writer and poet, he took it upon himself as a challenging, charitable, humanitarian task to be gentle and take it all in. This document of such is a testament to the departure into that otherwise world. It is so *there*.

And you can be there too. Either vicariously through this work, when you need a pick me up, or an attunement, or by lifting your wings and joining the frequency of: the airwaves, water waves, rock waves, breathing tree waves, bohemian party waves, in joining the parts of this Earth and country that exist in long time – rock time, desert time, sun time, forest time. Or human time, bird time, leaf time, road time. It's our time.

What I enjoyed with these haikus was the type of peace that waves bring; always rolling in, and lapping their way back out, and it doesn't quite matter when or where you step in. Each moment in time he sat propped or supported by a tree or rock. We have the opportunity to share that moment, and to see what was in the perspective, the panoramic, the type of time that you don't quite need to wait for to find. He draws on a tradition of both personal revelation with Nature and the cacophonous vibrations of travelers and humans in collaboration. We take in all that our senses and spirits can handle, and distill them, let moments speak to us, write it down, and pass it around. In this collection, the journey stretches from sea to sea, and encourages you to be with yourself and do the same.

These haikus are a breath of fresh air. So often

our reading demands rigorous intellectual engagement. The gentle distillations and age-old alchemies occurring all around us simply ask for us to embrace our sensual natures and tune in. Deerfield has created the station from which to do so, yet simultaneously acknowledges that these waves are not separate from the magic of everyday.

As we step into our working selves, our loving selves, our creative selves, our political selves, our nature-loving, wandering dream-punk selves, we realize just how much a part of the whole we truly are. We are moving into forgotten, yet reawakening territory in the land of self-love. When we remember to breathe, and let our eyes, hearts, ears, internal frequencies tune into the giant wave-like heartbeat of the planet and each other, there's no quite telling where we will go.

Yet for the moment, it is wonderful to just be.

Deerfield's gentle, discerning spirit shares all of this with us, so let's join him in his bum-clown car, and travel by haiku.

Stephanie B.
author of Letters To Aunt Lucy
January 2016

Travel by Haiku

Vol. 1: **The Sea, The Air, The Beaten Earth Road.**

Lost highways

American Dreams

the earth listens
as we hold our breath.

Now

breathe in the giant air

and expel all the fear that holds you back.

Adventure awaits

close your eyes
and breathe deeply
let your dreams take hold.

A west coast
highway
cut through Cascade
mountain range

ending at the sea.

Big Sur in spring
is even more
psychedelic
with succulent
blooms.

Hills that roll and make
you say "Wow!"
with all your
heart.
EARTH and SEA
that shouts!

Clouds of fog
floating
heavenly
above, dressing
the mountains in
awe.

Cliffs made of granite

ocean crashing upon them

restful Buddhas.

Standing with the tide

meditating
on the sea

rooted in the waves.

Rock
balance
valley

many earth meditations
laid against that sea.

<u>The Sea:</u> Never in any rush to get any place, but always on time.

The whole land is just a bunch of boulders that fell into that big sea.

Today,

I wrote about the sea,
and she came up
the shore

and

splashed

me.

Travel by Haiku

Vol. 2: **The Trees On The High Mountain Grow Tall.**

Appalachian
(high)way
winding
around
mountain bends
mind silent in
awe.

Blue mountain giants
          on every horizon
              belly up in dream.

          Great Smoky Mountains
only half there
in sleepy fog.

          Smoky Mountains
           smoky wet weather
snow in the mountain range.

The snow-capped mountains
whisper in the fog, saying:
"Breathe in the cold air.

"Be humble and watch.
The mountain breeze
carries with
it full refreshment.

"A mystic's knowledge
fed by all the
mountain's streams."
My heart runs zig-zags.

Sometimes **making love** consists of standing very still in a field and looking at the **ice fall onto a mountain top**.

A poet gathers
insight from the silent dark
atop the highlands.

Think of the mountain flower
its tiny beauty
hanging onto cliffside.

Meditate up high
watch the whole world
drift below
transcend your confines.

There's an openness to all of this. Keep still and watch the time flow by.

A grandfather clock
chimes on the mountain cliffside
but time is forgot.

Blue mountain ridges
ancient chief burial mounds
drifting through the clouds.

Riding the ridges
of a mountainous landscape
I find my silence.

"Silence comes easy,"
says the rustling of the leaves
in the quiet trees.

Magic really speaks
        in the mountains from every
bird and evergreen.

It's amazing how
        far out you can get when
driving down a mountain.

At the base of the
rockies, things start to get
a little weird.

Creatives seeping
out of mountain springs
from earth
the flow of culture.

Green earth, mountain still
free-thinking free atmosphere
skinny-dip your heart in it.

Dog covered in burs
smiling like on his birthday
spreading seeds of life.

Laying in green sun
feeling the grasshoppers bounce
taking it easy.

Found a penny in a hot spring
helluva day, man
we're all rich fishes, baby!

Lost highways
American
Dreams
Douglas Fir
alleyways to
the soul.

Impressive mountain
volcano erupting
live earth
where
redwood
grow tall.

Mount Shasta: reckless
yet settled, earth that vibrates,
a goddess to man.

She grows even
taller the more you
drive away from her.

The clouds overhead
Shasta shouts up at that sky
envious for it.

Climbing half a peak
to get a better view of
    the surrounding range.

(It doesn't take much to climb a granite
mountain with the right boots on.)

Mountain for miles
sunset goes even longer
    with all the ripples.

The sun sets long after the
    sun disappears
behind the mountains.

Mountain top
elliptical
   sun running in
               circles
      magic
      meditation
ritual by day
and night.

Big sky on
mountains

sun rises and
sun sets

there's romance
in nature.

Fine time to find
a redwood grove
bathed in
summer

sunset
afterglow.

We sleep nestled in
with giants glowing under
golden rays of light.

A little redwood
            faerie ring forms
                        and
        soaks up the moonlight.

The Moon Queen
raising that beautiful
golden glow
the humble redwoods,
her home.

Head high in
the clouds
climbing the
literal wind
she carries the
earth.

We sleep in gold needles
redwood towering above
forest floor is silent.

A walk with dinosaurs
sleeping in old subway cars
made of fallen wood.

Inside the heart of
an elder, I find my voice
with ease.

The woods, they call out a humble chorus.

The trees, they creak in the wind.

"You don't need to make art. The redwood tree is enough art already."

"There are secrets in these **redwoods** that only the trees themselves can tell."

"The magic
of a tree
is looking up at it.

Stand back and
stare up!"

"Height awakens peace of mind, of spirit.

Look up!

See?

An ancient remedy."

"Stand in awe. Height so tall, it will make you question your reality."

The grandmother of all these
trees must be one hell of a tall
lady...

Here she is: the national
heavyweight champion.
Any thoughts?

*Lying below her, it's a wonder,
but what of flying, like Crow,
around her?*

Imagine the woods
without trees. Then
where would you
stand tall and look up?

Earth awakens the mystery
we all hold within our
swollen trunks.

Ages of sorrows
held tightly within the bark
a tree grows outwards.

If a tree falls in
the woods and I hear it,
did it really happen?

The clown bum pursuit
of becoming a redwood
can also be silly.

The tree so big it
falters in its growth. Raven
calls out for daylight.

Sun shining through the
trees and coming out so bright
in the undergrowth.

Take notice of the fresh air
and red amber
seeping in with the sun
through the branches.

A tall redwood grove
bursts with random connections
broken paths unite.

Man stood in these woods forty thousand years ago.

Not too much has changed.

Travel by Haiku

Vol. 3: **In The Desert Am I Lost For Good?**

A desert road
sign reads like a
poet's mantra:

**"Slow down
and enjoy the
view."**

Buttes cast **in shadow
warm sun**, blue sky,
and soft clouds
this
desert morning.

Local birds migrate
**south with the warm
breeze,**
little wings flicker
delight.

Desert birds chirping
greeting the pleasant sunshine
with beauty and abundance.

Canyon sparrows fly
southwest following the wind
into the badlands.

In South Dakota
the pheasant floats through
cornfields
on psychedelic colored wings.

I watched a
crow fly
into the
pueblo ruins
and come out a
man.

Badlands

Native lands
spirit of ancient
wanders

here still strong today.

I feel the
ancients
I feel their
forgotten souls
their footprints
etched in
sandstone.

Delicate arches
worn out by time's
erosive,
    sensitive nature.

Arches as windows
or portals to spirit worlds
and ancient timelines.

The Joshua Trees
    as human contortionists
    reborn as weird trees.

Their arms held
outstretched.
  Yucca are like young Shivas,
dancing in the desert flames.

The mysticism
of   now.

Trapped forever
in
desert paradise.

Lost tribes
traveling
the space

between present and
a past forgotten.

Soft rock and carved stone

gives a lot of new meaning

to life's sweet shortness.

The valley narrows
two canyons converge
to one
I slip through the cracks.

Palm fronds in the wind
boulders on the horizon
desert **oasis**.

Beer combined
with heat

makes Señor Deerfield
complete,

A (desert) jester
for all.

There is poetry on my lips. It
tastes like
     rock salt and glycerin:

Sweet desert mamas
    looking fine under big skies
      giving me heat stroke.

The sun tans my legs
and sand burns my pretty feet
     as I escape certain death.

Along the prairie
wind blows
without direction
and life
springs to life.

Small desert quail
  feasting on seeds found in sand
     chirping with delight.

Tiny lizard hugs
tall tree and nods his small head
flaunting his colors.

Desert floor
rumbles
clouds in the
sunshine
peace atop the
cliffs.

Cowboy sits asleep
    brushing off desperate
                    flies
        dodging direct sun.

Scavenger poets,
 we make great travelers
grabbing words from the
                    sand.

*The sand turns
pink now*

like the desert sun

*setting into the
mountains.*

If you stay still for **long enough** the spectacle comes naturally.

Multi-colored air
        desert in Technicolor
valley on fire.

Sun-sky gradient
    changing between energies
warm and cold, pinks...blues.

            Valley of fire
    ancient sea, unraveled stone
hypnotic color.

A lone hiker
walks
the sand blows
west with the
wind.

otherwise, silence.

Silence of desert
empty open
universe
space beyond the
void.

The boulders pile high
the stars open for
business
in deep purple skies.

The sweet desert haze
swallowing everything
in purple currents.

The beating
heart of
our country
sits at the
center of it
and waits.

Travel by Haiku

Vol. 4: **I Am The Rain, We Are The Cosmos.**

The rain follows me
making the
landscape turn green
feeding my inner spring child.

Passing rain shower
so modest in composure
the gift of fresh dew.

The way metal sounds
when rained on
or the dogs' barks in
a playful fight.

A rainy day in May.
  Seemed like a good day to go
       into a cave.

So much wonder and
   mystery. What a timeless
   dream within a dream.

Why did Dali care so much
about rhino horns?
       Look at stalactites!

Underground selfie

NARCISSISM

even in the lowest
of depths.

To the headwaters
　　we journey back to our roots
　　　　craving energy.

From another realm
　　comes water for the surface
　　　　giving land its life.

River turned to mud
　tree bent sideways by the storm
　　the world grows askew.

Seasons turn over
summer born out
of the spring
and **the earth
stays green**.

From sweet
mountain
spring

youth finds an entry point,

and restores
our lifeforce.

Middle earth water
rushes from the gateway to
Mount Shasta's chakra.

Slept in a field made
of stars. Woke up to music,
circus, and warm chai.

Hearing rush and flow
from headwaters that feed a state.
I   enter   dream.

A creative space
set by a river
springing
writers,
song,
and dance.

Elven butterflies
and hippy children
gather round the cold waters.

Faeries and serpents
found in grass by the river
strumming harps and hearts.

Simple butterfly
soaring at the headwaters
heart beating happy.

The wind redirects
aims for the banjo player
        and carries his notes.

            River faerie harp
    taking a dip in the stream
vibrating the space.

Hippy river cove,
        it's got the mojo working
        ❥ heart beats ecstatic
(with blues music vibes).

Forever lounging
riding the day's
ebb and flow

summer
mountain
spring.

Slowly fading down
the sun takes its good ole' time
letting nighttime grow.

A gracious sunset
Yosemite stands silent
gratitude up high.

A tiny finger
nail of a new moon appears, just
as the sun goes down.

The new moon rises
        a sliver of abundance
casting a shadow.

Now, that new moon caught
in some evergreens, careful
she don't catch fire.

The **cool reflection** in a holy alpine lake changes perspectives.

The Milky Way glows brighter, **the longer you look at it**, the later it gets.

Suddenly the stars are out, full
glow, the cosmos illuminated.

Night's cold slipping in
        over high sierra trail
and onto my page.

So many airplanes
zigzag overhead
        not knowing what lies below.

How far out is it
to think:

SPACESHIP
EARTH

passing
through a cloud of
meteors.

We tiny space men
drifting across
the planet

and time
driving by.

The same granite hill
a wholly different sunset
still, a great moment.

A wind blows
through Tioga Pass
gracing the trees below
with fresh alpine air.

The moon blowing
a kiss in the clouds
she shines through.

Good thing this
planet goes round.
The sun is
always
setting
somewhere,
everywhere.

The fish start to jump
at midnight, hoping to catch
some late evening dreams.

Steady now, the cliffs
hold much magic when looking
down into the lake.

Dreams of the bottom
of Crater Lake, covered in
blues from inner worlds.

Moon light,
moon vision
water is all
around us
tidal waves within.

The river and its handshake

with the
full   moon.

Taking all the time
    to watch the waterfall
        beneath a waterfall.

Water falls, rocks fall
    reaching equilibrium
face of the cliff, changed.

Stream Meditation:
    Waterfalls cut at the rock
between   blue   mountains.

There is one **song** to the waterfall

made up of so **many voices**.

The river still chatters to me
even when
I barely listen.

The thoughtful tree
at the base of a waterfall:

Stay still and watch the
groundhog cross the river rocks
minding his balance.

I understand god(s)...

They exist within all of this. They exist in us all.

Travel by Haiku

Vol. 5: **City Slicking And Chasing The Sun.**

I don't think there's too many poets to have driven across the country with an old busted TV, a suitcase full of dream catchers, a small busking amp, a unicorn mask and the accompanying trumpet, a bunch of camping gear, road bike strapped to the back, a glove compartment full of incense, 3 pairs of aviator sunglasses, and 6 data CDs of Fela Kuti to keep the vibes flowing. If only that's all I brought, this car would be a lot emptier. Here's to the memories! See you all later! Keep in touch. Stay tuned. Drop out. Join me.

Made it to Baltimore after nightfall. Friend I haven't seen in a year answered the door, just back from a 10-day meditation retreat. We talked about minds and silence and inner awakenings and alternate realms until our other friends came home and took me away to a record release party at the Copycat with Soft Cat leading the night full of old friends, good lighting and wandering vibes. Shared some haiku sigils with a group of strangers after one of them asked what my henna tattoo meant. Everyone so friendly and rose petals strewn along the floor. A tiredness along the night air but there's plenty of couches to lay back on and get cozy. It gets friendly as you travel south!

Homes made of color
city of raven poems
psychedelic grounds.

Spring found in a field
of tulips growing beside
the B-more highways.

In DC I led an entire living room of strangers in howling at the mother moon. It happened spontaneously out of a reading of a short story titled, *The Full Moon in SF*. The second time that happened this tour. There was a collaboration between myself and a dancer and an upright bassist. Together we made the sun rise. A living room with my dream body Ma Ja Ka, the magical unicorn, and an interpretive play, with 70 or 80 concert goers all squeezed in so tight some people stood outside and looked through the windows, even I felt like I was dreaming.

U Street has changed a lot since I first stumbled down these darkened roads for a show at the Black Cat, the only soul on the road, understanding first hand why the punks here used to say DC stood for "Dead City". Now it's shape shifting with gentrification and tons of commercial life, and not always the most diverse kind, but at the moment you think there's too many wine bars or dress shops, you round the corner and there is a live graffiti jam posting up in some alleyway and then

there's a jazz bar called Bohemian Cavern
across the street and a poetry joint a
few blocks away pumping Fela Kuti over the
overhead speakers. The faces are diverse
and the voices are mixing and blending.

Even Ben's Chili Bowl is adapting
opening a cocktail lounge next door, and
when I peak in to see what it's like, I
see it's definitely not a dive, but the
people inside still look very humble on
this pleasant Sunday afternoon. There's
culture holding on and people thinking
about their roots and though I'm sure
everyone's rent check is skyrocketing, and
I notice there's a fair share of homeless
and crazy being ignored, it seems like
maybe the community has figured out how to
stay active and connected and grounded,
welcoming in all these new faces, and perhaps
sculpting a new American dream together.

I'm a dreamer and sometimes I tell
hyperbole but it really is interesting
to see all of these different types of
people sharing a city block, some of
them it's their home and others are just
visiting for the beer gardens, but all

of them are getting along and filling the
neighborhood with their multi-cultural
vibes, maybe not even self aware.

Settling into that easy southern
good times flow
sundown with river birds.

Change on every corner
pennies and even quarters
this Richmond is a goldmine!

I read in Richmond as the rain poured outside with the essence of love-making, flooding the streets with cool natural air and cherry blossoms floating in these newborn streams.

One woman wrote my words on her legs and arms in permanent ink as I read aloud and the calligraphy smeared and splattered across the canvas of her skin as she tried to keep pace with my voice. When I finished, I had to rouse my audience out of the dream space I had crafted for them. I sold dream catchers and mixtapes and people talked about how my writing style reminded them of their own painting process.

I find I've been very collaborative lately, more so perhaps than ever before. A woman told me of this film she's been working on, a play that takes place inside her vagina and she asked me to be a part of it. She'll use green screens and other effects to make a stage out of her sex for the performances to take place within. Imagine that, Ma Ja Ka ... a unicorn playing the trumpet in the entryway to the womb. I can't make this stuff up. A friend gave me two pieces of orgonite he made, one for my cellphone and one for my heart. I also got a piece of Egyptian Quartz. And now I'm driving to North Carolina listening to mountain music and feeling more awake, the greener it gets.

Heavy clouds hang high
    color of ash in the sky
        quiet mountain town.

So many small streams
chattering away, forming
    meditative sounds.

    The French Broad River
quiet, yet proud of her curves
        so old and
        rhythmic.

This tiny bubble of psychedelia, stuck between mountain ranges with dream punks and astral projections and prohibition era steamboat tramps. Every bar named after a poet and the views all over of these large green black mountains holding the clouds over their heads.

Surprisingly dense
with mountain folks and artists
tramps and vagabonds.

Home of healing arts
overtop large quartz crystal
focal point of love.

Since I've hit the south the Masons and psychic vampirism have been consistent topics of conversation. And here I am this bumbling fool unicorn just passing through. I say my words and play my trumpet and I lower myself from the traditional writer's pedestal enough so that we can all talk casual when I finish. It helps that I'm a punk and it helps I'm doing readings at houses and small art galleries. I ride my bike and I feel lucky to still feel grounded as opposed to being swept away in a whirlwind of pre-existing emotion and doubt. The interesting thing about running into the grandson of a Freemason ultimate wizard or whatever you would call the Sith Lord equivalent of being on top, is that even they are attempting to use their inherited power to create good in a world that is being torn apart by the old generation's misguided practices of burn and pillage. It's interesting to hear about their battles and their constant struggles with these dark forces that are still trying to dominate the social consciousness. Things like social

Darwinism and "every man for himself". It's amazing what can be created when even these people of power redirect their efforts towards beauty and community. It's a whole new vocabulary and it begs the question of what the next generation's leaders are going to look like. Will we even have leaders then? Or will everyone just exist in tiny bubble communes making things work locally?

We also talk about how Netflix is killing house shows. So many people stuck behind their TV monitors catching up on the latest series as opposed to going out and seeing some culture.

Green hills like
Scotland
thunder clapping
against it.
Georgian
spring
downpour.

I started out this trip with one of my haikus:

The sand turning pink
like the desert sun
setting into the mountains.

tattooed on the back of my hand as a sigil in the form of an arrow pointing forward, though the artist's intention was for it to point inward. Over the week it has served its purpose guiding me forward on the road with the necessary flow to get me there, and then it gradually faded leaving me to turn to my own personal magic and power to stay afloat. I typewrite poetry on the street for interested tourists and fellow travelers and read it at night to small gatherings in bars and living rooms, exchanging my dream labors for donated currency and couches to sleep upon. Without my feet tethered down to any one location I find myself adrift through a sea of various characters and personalities all revealing themselves to me through conversations on dreams and a sharing of self-revelations. We examine the human mystery and aspire to the occult. Running in the same circles, it was only a matter of time before we stumbled into each other's present moment. And here I am, I have gotten to the point in the trip where new faces appear familiar, reminding me sometimes of those I know from home, and we exchange dialogue as if we have known each other for a long time finding comfort in each other's company. There is no end to this joy of meeting strangers I know. All this and I continue with the same resolve, a journey forward with the spring rain clouds pummeling the increasingly green southeastern terrain under my feet, thunder clapping at my back, a knapsack strung over my shoulders, and that beauty of the muse frequenting my conscious mind and perhaps awakening inside my heart the further out I go. Actually, I've caught glimpses of her now getting ever closer, hanging around the outer edge of each audience, smiling and nodding her head as I speak her dedication, snapping her fingers to my haikus, and laughing as the whole room fills with wild wolves howling out her icaros mantra,

"Hoooowwww? Ow! Ow! Owww! Hoooowww!!!"

I figure if I keep it going, it won't be too long before she meets me on this country's other side. And when I find her there, I will lie down a humble mountain perfectly glad to have the fortune to be here now and breathing alive.

Spring fertility
southern hospitality
Athens wanderlust.

City keeps sprawling
biking through outer farmlands
in abundant sunshine.

That **hippy lady**, she smiled at me, driving her little Cadillac.

Now in Atlanta, I find out there's a tree in Athens *that owns itself* and I'm bummed not to have seen it but still feeling pretty good after the hike along the river in the sun shower thunder storms. This after hanging out at a gallery show in the middle of the dregs of downtown. Outside felt kind of dire, but inside was covered in tie-dyed paint and layers of polka dotted murals. The show was upstairs but I got to explore the rest of the floors, about 5 of them, some underground, each themed a different way, and some only living rooms or living spaces while others these big huge venues for whatever crazy show is coming through. The place felt like Willy Wonka's castle, but I was careful not to lick the walls because I still had places to go. I follow some new friends made in Athens back to East Atlanta, which is a lot more residential and let the highway pass us by as we got higher watching Prince Rama music videos on a projector. Everyone friendly and some of them the funniest people I've ever met, in a southern surrealist way, and people asking me what people in Philadelphia are like and me telling them we're all assholes but in an honest way, and this one guy saying he traveled for a long time and he's pretty happy to not be traveling any time again soon and us talking about Montana ghost towns and oil booms. I wake up the next morning and bike around finding these tiny cultural bubbles maybe only a block or two wide but dotted around the city with murals and psychedelic vibes and coffee shops and bars and then surrounded by residential areas or sometimes just farmland the further out I get until at some point I'm biking up to a farmer's market the size of your average super Walmart and it's got all this fresh produce from all around and it's packed with all these normal people eating organic and having access to cheap good raw food. It feels American dream worthy and the sun is warm and I feel content to buy a baguette and make a French style sandwich before heading further back into the friendly decadence of the city's downtown.

Atlanta, full of
green spaces, and these
psychedelic trees.

Desperate city center
harsh vibes in this part of town
watch your step and find
some cents.

Last night, I read with a bunch of house poets and a psychedelic shaman inside a Dionysian pleasure palace of leisurely vibes and OG hippy radicalism. I've really felt inspired by all these places and people I've spent time with. It's just like always: I get on the road and here I am finding all these far out zones bubbling with creativity and alternative power. And people have been saying I've been inspiring right back at them. **To inspire and be inspired.** That always feels nice. And the main motif is all of these alternative spaces coming out of winter dormancy and feeling the renewing energy of spring, as I rearrange their living rooms and play a projection of a Yosemite waterfall above my TV altar.

The house poets now casting their spells and the shaman chanting his icaros while removing his mask. And then I'm lounging all day, following the sun like a cat to different rooms and eventually outside chatting with the Big House residents about the various ways to keep a commune organized and enjoying listening to their soft tranquil voices as they tell stories about living in Mexico City and how the artists there combat the cartels with the magic of a paintbrush. We are all really driven people taking the time to enjoy the sun. We sit on a back porch and climb up on top of the roof and talk about building treehouses with hammocks inside, then we move to the garden, and again we're on a porch being followed all the time by the chickens who enjoy our company but won't let us pet them. This and then I have to go again and get on the road, up and over the lush green of these Georgian and then Alabaman hills where there's probably more than a few wizened indigenous chieftains buried underneath these short friendly mounds.

Greek mythology
found in
Birmingham
hilltops
Vulcan, **green
and lush**.

In Birmingham, I listened to the trains pass by in every direction, as I biked around these great orbits in a southern graveyard in order to meet up with a fellow space traveler on the outer rings of Saturn. Space is the place. And I'm feeling weightless.

Rest in Power, Sun Ra.

The days of spring rain have followed me to New Orleans, transforming from mountain drizzle and swampy trickles into daily thunderstorms that rage against the city slums with such ferocity, I can only imagine what it would feel like to have to brace myself against a hurricane that hit.

The streets fill with water and the bayou heat breaks, everyone dabbing the sweat off their foreheads with handkerchiefs, the torrents of gulf rain pounding against the aluminum roofing. At a moment of extreme intensity the power blacks out and the thunder claps loudly above. Everyone in this creole cafe shouts with ooo's and ah's but before there's time to find a fuse to switch, the power is back on, Jazz Fest returns to the overhead radio, and everyone continues on with their by and large normal leisurely New Orleans days.

Crescent city voodoo
debauchery on the
streets
life free from restraint.

The swampy weather
makes the people big
babies
infinite childhood.

Some guy told me that New Orleans is a
Scorpio city. I told him I haven't been
stung yet. I've seen the stinger but never
taken it through the heart. He says you
never see it until it hits you. But I think
he's lying as I sit in a bedroom with a
full jazz band made up of two house poets
and whoever can play from the audience
joining them while the second loft of the
room paints their naked bodies, tracing
their beautiful curves in war paint and
the third loft above stares down painting
the entire thing on their canvases. The
musicians stare upwards and I move into
the next room following more sounds of
jazz and easy vibrations into the front
living room watching collaboration erupt
from the night sky. I'm thinking of nothing
other than this mansion is a powerhouse
with so much culture it overflows into the
alleyways and there's so much color and
psychedelic aspirations and people just

finding their oneness, I'm a poet and I can't think straight following the upright bass and beat of the drums. There's drunk in the room and then there's dream and these people frolic between the outer realms of existence and the things that make the creative being full (flow).

Oh, voodoo love child lay it on me baby, nice I'm all for chaos.

There're tornadoes down here in New Orleans, rolling off the lake and pushing a whole freight train off its track. Up in Baltimore there's another group of police officers not convicted after murdering a fellow brother, but they don't get off completely because the whole city rises up in protest announcing they just can't take it anymore, smashing cop cars and bank windows until this brutality stops and thankfully continuing this national dialogue that needs to keep happening for things to actually change.

Black Lives Matter! they chant.

Over in Nepal there are earthquakes caterwauling against civilization sinking whole villages in the uproar and one can only hope there's some humanitarian aide sent to all those now in need.

And anyone seen that volcano down in Chile, angry as the first day she breathed? She's been going off for several days now filling the skies with molten rock and storm clouds of ashen fury.

Some days, they have more cataclysm than others, especially in today's modern times where headlines are world-centric and not just local and introverted. On all days though, there's this mighty Mississippi which now sits in front of me cutting through our country's heart, vicious and unrelenting, poisoned waters that are dangerous to taste, overflowing her bounds. She's a true devil if there ever was one. And it's okay because upon her banks sits an abandoned warehouse, turned to condos, with big roll-paint block letters up the brick side, spelling out:

"You are beautiful", just as a reminder in case you or she or anyone else forgot.

For almost three weeks I've been driving
due south but today, I'm heading west.
I've forgotten what it feels like to chase
the sun or how it feels to cross a time
zone and all the sudden gain an extra hour
of day. My heart bubbles in anticipation
of the Texan sunset about to be in front
of me and me driving into it expecting a
pot of gold or some other affirmation of
traveling the distance.

What will the legend of **Ma Ja Ka be after** all these travels are over?

Marshall Deerfield is Marshall James Kavanaugh in poetic form. His travels take him to places only the subconscious can sometimes understand.

When he's not on the road he can usually be found in the Philadelphia area with his two cats, building large TV installations.

photo by Tara Lynn Faith Williamson

Other Titles Available from

A Freedom Books:

www.afreedombooks.com

About the Cover

The cover of this book was designed by Marshall James Kavanaugh. The background is a photo of a sunset witnessed in Joshua Tree National Park in California. The sunset went on for hours and it felt like the entire desert woke up to its brilliance.

There is nothing like the sunsets in Joshua Tree.

Tune into Haiku TV:

<u>marshalljameskavanaugh.com/haiku-tv.html</u>

The haikus in this book, when performed live, are accompanied by TV installations and video art. These devices create the atmosphere to experience the space between each line of a haiku. The chapter headers for each section are but a small sampling of the audio/visual components available to you.

Follow the link above to deepen your journey.

Acknowledgements

Thank you to everyone who hosted me along the way in my travels. To my family and to all the friends that I acquired in my journeys across the country. For everyone who shared a haiku with me or gave me words of inspiration or motivated me to go out and see the world. I offer my upmost gratitude to you.

Special thanks to: Mom, Dad, Karen, Zef, Stephanie B., Gus, Andrew G., Tara & Shane, Rebecca G., Cameron S. Marian and Vianney and The Holy Underground, John and Kelsey and Chris, Mariah, Courtney Blue, Sage, Lady Laura, Erin W., Johnny Fantastic, Mary C., Citron, Josie, Talon, Jeff Blinder, Logan S., Scott C., Nicole B., Nath an, Kelly Ann, Maizy and Gary, Catherine R., Milton, Alex Z., Cat Ries, Edwin and Chelsea, Bradley, Frank Hurricane, Giusseppe, Bonnie C., Radek, Jordan, Gracie, Chris M., Megan Wood, Camilla, Tom V., John Tucker, Bobby Wasabi and Julia, Tanner, Grace T., Nico and Diana, Spencer, Matthew H., Pauly K., Hunter, Sean L., Adam S., Claire B., Tim Hale, Alex Baker, Amanda P., Uncle Bill, Cousin Jill, Alexia and Julia, & so many more.